Neo-Marxist Realism

The problem of democrady is who will guard the guardians.Mass democracy is colonized by the mass media.

The weaknesses of democracies of the West are conspicuous.All the social groups should be held accountable by the media and take part in the political proccess.

The army ,the police and the industrialists will negotiate with the government for power and privileges and those negotiations should be known to the journalists.

The open question is why the newspapers don't write about the military and the business since they are political actors.What law prohibits real freedom of speech.

Some questions ,the media didn't answer.Who are the cleptocrats?

A new work ethic is needed to overcome economic depression.Legitimization of donations to politicians.

The managerial politics and the idealism of new vision.The nationalists had the idealism to protect the national interests.

A superb opportunity to express a modern national vision of progress,beyond the simple managerial administration that lets the events to pass by, without creating political thinking or building the national future on the foundations of positive ethicological values.

The Greek philosophy was allways ethicological and value driven .It is our duty to continue this tradition.The multiple collectiveness is a characteristic of strong government structures.

For a new political party to establish itself ,it has to be based on positions and ideological foundations,not in a personality cult without the depth of political creativity.

The usuring capital want Greece to go bankrupt.Drastic solutions are needed for the defense of the nation.The creation of a small public sectorin Greece,must happen as soon as possible, to avoid the risk of bankruptcy.

The mass media have to control not only the political establishment but also the other pillars of power ,the military and the industry.A question remains.

Why the money have to be managed by the cleptocrats?Where do they come from?They are the persons who profited the most and became billionaires the last two decades.

In Greece the bureaucracy has a mentality of

corruption.The persons who work in the public sector consider themselves,like in other Orthodox countries,the elite of the nation ,a special interest group that all the politicians have to depend on if they want the government to function.

They created an excessive debt for the public sector,by being bribed from foreign corporations.Those corporations grabbed the Greek money,which the Greeks borrowed from foreign banks and they didn't use to build an exporting business as they should.

The discovery of minerals in Afghanistan is the guarantee that the Americans will stay there,because they will have economic profits from their exploitation.If they didn't have profits they would have to withdraw from Iraq and Afghanistan because the rise of the public debt would be meteoric.

The problem with the Greek billionaires is that they never understood they have the obligation to give something back to the community,for example an industrial base.

They just collect the money and put it in their Swiss bank accounts.They didn't offer anything to the Greek society.The wealthy persons of the world have to accept a new social contract.

It will state that the creation of an industrial base will create jobs and social responsibility is to build hospitals and schools.

And to give financial help to the weaker segments of society.If that doesn't happen the future will be different than we expect.

With economic deppression destroying employing opportunities and wealth ,totalitarian regimes will emerge where the buraeucratic insitutions will control social life and democracy will be extinct

The growth of the economy is essential to keep and expand the democratic values.The capitalist must be obliged to be a humanist.Otherwise the hatred of hungry masses will haunt him.We can find the Golden rule if we study incentive theory game theory and microeconomics.

The problematic behavior of the labor unions which go on strikes is conspicuous.The human effort to control.

It is prefferable for reasons of long term growth and stability,the center of power to be the employer and not the emploee.Because the workers care only about their interests,they overcharge the corporation and do insufficient work.

They create debt,losses and low competitiveness for corporations and states.Whoever is the owner of a thing will have to obey to the laws of economics and give something only in exchange of a service.

The same principle applies to those who control the global flow of money. They sell money. The merchants of cash.

They will not give away cash even to their closest relative, without asking for a return. The billionaires of the world have to answer a few questions.

Why they have to own so much money?What law made it so?Who manages their money?How they gained control of their fortune,if not with some kind of stealing.Experts like lawyers and economists will manage the big corporations and the profits will return to the citizens,because they will be shareholders of the state.

A military revolution will bring the Neo-Marxists into power.When all the developed nations ,like the USA and the UK,have so great public debt they will drown in it.

Even these nations which are the bases of the global banking capital will be forced to reexamine if the power of banks is good for them.The curent global system of power is based on the designs of bankers to establish their rule and to preserve it for centuries.But when the wave of the masses turns against them pushed by debts and poverty their praetorians will have to abandon them in their fate and take the side of the people.

When the superpower declares bankruptcy people will question,who are these bankers,why they operate in secrecy and who covers them?

The military and the police of great nations will have to support the abolition of loans and debt and the stop of banking activities as we know them today.

The bankers and the plutocrats can lose their

position overnight.A new system will be born.

All the profits of the corporations will be redistributed to the global citizens.The corporations will be managed by experts and noone will have more money than a limit.

Everyone will take their share of the profits.The commercial banks will be abolished.The same will happen with usury and giving loans with an interest.

Only a central bank will exist for every nation which will give money without interest and often will give money for free,to develop the industry and technology or even to help consumption.All debts public and private will be abolished as the law will declare.

Everyone will have the necessary to survive and will work in jobs that complete them as personalities.

They will earn more money from their jobs to increase the consumption.

This political system can be named Liberal Marxism or Neo-Marxist Realism.

When this system is established as a global governing system in the USA and UK that will be the real end of history.

The nations that will adopt this system of governance will give liberty and strength to their citizens.

The rest of the world will suffer from unequal distribution of wealth which causes unequality in social position.

The dialectics or the conflict between nations will continue because of human nature.

But nations will be more equal than before.Billionaires and the system that created them will be abolished.

Everyone will earn wha they really deserve.The

new system will function better in a secularized society Interest rates will stop to exist.

All citizens will be equal.The corporations will not have shareholders.Some individuals will live better because of their intellectual achievement.The most educated and the experts will rule.

The revolution of the army will happen in highly indebted nations like Greece,which has to write off its foreign debt and the private debt to the commercial banks which will have to close.

They will forbid the banks to operate in the country.A new independent central bank will be founded and it will create new currency that it will give where it is needed without interest rate.This central bank will finance the industrial base.

Other nations will follow the success of Greece.The central bank of a nation with the new system will belong to the people and not to the state or to some families.

Every citizen from the time he or she is born until death will be a shareholder in the central bank and in the industries and will take dividend from their operation.

Private property will be allowed until the limit of seven million dollars per person. The rest of the profits will go to the state budget for public projects.

When the military understands,probably pushed by the masses,that the abandoment of capitalism which favors only the old families and is controlled by them ,is the solution to the global problem of poverty and will favor the existence of the armed forces in power.They will agree with Ne0-Marxist Realism.

Every country that adopts the new system will be free and independent.The masses of plebes will transform into citizens co-owners of the state who will decide by voting in a Swiss model about all the public issues.The money that the central bank will create will be property of the citizens.

The present system of organized monetary and

political administration,is not a God-given law,it is only an accounting alchemy designed to serve only a few families of bankers.

With a new system design we can bring freedom and equality to the tribes.

They will create communities free from the burden of debt.They will live in their own way of life.

In theory,today anyone has the liberal right to become rich.The dark reality is that you have to be a member of a secret society to achieve affluence.A revolution against debt will succeed only if the armed forces support it.The polticians will have to follow the popular demand for radical change.

If other nations declare war on Greece to steal more money from her we have to develop the defense industry to fight them.

The game to help both of the opponents to fight each other is the method to control the outcome.Only the insiders know the real purpose of the game organizer.

Greece will be a model state and others will follow her steps.

The new system will be named revolutionary Neo-Marxist Realism.

Secret senarios want Greece to be a geopolitical satellite of Turkey in the next twenty years.

The two pillars or columns of the new regime will be the militants and the workers.When the debts of the Western nations become so large,the impoverished masses will revolt against the banks and everyone who supports their rule.

Global usurers are the tyrants of mankind.The mediocre of the known families rule today the world.

A different tommorow may emerge when we teach the people that they are equal or better than the so called aristocracy and when they decide to take away the power of usury from the hands of bankers.

The existence of billionaires should be

prohibited by law.Any political party from the Left to the Right can start the Neo-Marxist Realistic revolution.

Because it is the only solution to the problem of many nations.

A Neo-Marxist society will create the new human-citizen who will be equal.He will have higher ethics and aesthetics.A society of philosophers will be created where everyone ,by having solved the problem of survival will live his or her life by completing his or her personality with education and with playing games.

A scientific revolution will follow,new inventions in genetic improvement of humans will be quickly adopted because a secularized mentality will prevail.

The restraints of religion hold back scientific research for no logical reason.The church was allways an enemy of science.

Humans will be free.Exploitation and slavery will end forever.An important aspect of establishing the new state is to persuade the militants that the new system is beneficial for the survival and progress of the nation.And that will happen when the debt will be so heavy upon the industrialized nations that wide masses of citizens will demand the end of bankers and banks.At that critical moment the army must be closer to the people and they have to understand that stability and progress will endure only with the new regime.At the same time the bankers may attempt to establish totalitarian police states and to end democracy because everyone would vote against the politicians they chose.The politicians who are chosen from the citizens will be forced to accept the new philosophy of administration because of unprecedented events.

The debt crisis of capitalism must bring a revolution of Neo-Marxist Realism. The issue of corporate profits and its practical value for the masses.

In the managed economy there will be central planning of industrial production depending on the needs of the nation.If a factory doesn't have profits but produces something usefull,will take capital from the central bank without interest to continue its function.Because of the ansense of interest rates inflation will be nonexistent.

An influx of foreign workers will occur.They

will have a lower legal status than a normal citizen.

Because the citizens as co-owners of the state will be millionaires foreign labour force will enter the country to do the lower jobs.The corporate profits will be distributed to the citizens.

The citizens will have the freedom to own land and medium size businesses.

The nation under the rule of the new regime will have to be ready for war with the armies of the previous creditors.

The simple but important move to close the banks and to delete all debts will free humanity from the teeth of the usurers who suck their blood.

The rise of an individual in the social ladder will be based on merit and not on which family he comes from.

Equal opportunities will exist for everyone. We will establish direct democracy. Every citizen will vote electronically about all the public issues.

The polticians willexplain the issues to the citizens.The citizens will create the new laws.

Individual liberties are essential for this system to succeed.

Laissez faire capitalism created the corrupted individual with low ethics.

The law about unjustified wealth takes away the right to become rich that in theory exists in the West for everyone.It makes people counterproductive.The invisible hand of capitalism is a big lie.The ancient families and their agents direct the global economy.There is secret central planning.

Chinese communism could become the next political system for export to other nations.

China has high growth rates with low debt.Its success may lead to Marxist transformations in European nations and political institutions of the West.

A government of national unity can implement the program of Neo-Marxist Realism.

Races can be equal only if the have economic equality.

Inflation will become extinct when speculation and bank usury become illegal.The law will predict stable prices at an objective level.The end of the Euro currency will come.

The experiment of euro will be over.We can have

Marxism without refusing modern liberties.

The Russian communist model of dictatorship of the proletariat failed

Because it didn't evolve into a classless society as Marx had predicted.Capitalism degrades humans.Capitalism turns them into animals who have to fight for their daily meal.Laissez faire capitalism doesn't guarantee anything,not even the basic need for survival.

The kings and queens of the world through a piece of crumbs to the poor masses and the worker has to be obliged because they allow him to exist.

Humanity is a slave to the capitalists in the present

system.Mass democracy is a lie.An oligarchy with friendly fascism is the real regime.

The rich people like to laugh at the misery of the unlucky.In the capitalist social Darwinic model the human has to be the fittest to survive to become accepted.The fact that he is a human and he deserves the help of society to live is not enough for this model of covered fascism.

The relation of production creates the human character.The end of the markets as a governing institution will come to an end.

The fall of communism in the Soviet Union and eastern Europe was a victory of the bankers.

Marxism never failed as a political philosophy.Only the particular experiment in Russia has failed.

Marxism in the future must be mixed with liberalsism and realismin order to succeed.In the future political parties will prevail if they address the masses as a whole and not a particular segment of society.

With today's standards the human is only usefull as a consumer and a worker.The revolution will free humans.

In the final stage machines will replace workers.Humanity will be free to enjoy life.

Marxism must be combined with hedonism and a Messianic vision of the end of history.The modern human can never be persuaded to follow an aschetic form of Marxism.

The state has to end as an independent entity.The Will of the people will control directly the government functions with voting.

USA will be the first nation to accept Neo-Marxist Realism .Other nations will follow.